Talk About It

Andresha Scott

Presentation by *BookLeaf Publishing*

Web: www.bookleafpub.com

E-mail: info@bookleafpub.com

ISBN: 9789357617734

First edition 2023

This book is dedicated to my girls,

*My best friend Temila Dent and my little sister
LaCrecia Hill. I thank God for allowing me to
have them in my life. They were the ones I could
"talk about it" with. We shared every secret
with one another. They held on to my secrets
and I to theirs.*

Missing them is an understatement...

ACKNOWLEDGEMENT

First and foremost, I want to take time out to thank God, for without Him none of what I do or have would be possible. He called me out of a life that was headed to nowhere and shaped and molded me into the person that I am today. I give Him all the glory and honor.

I'm eternally grateful to my mother, as a single mother she sacrificed a lot to raise my siblings and me. She taught me discipline, tough love, manners, respect, and so much more that has helped me succeed in life. I truly have no idea where I'd be if she would have given up on me.

To my sibling, we have been through so much as a unit, but I thank God for them. They were my first friends, first fights, and the first people to have my back. We are not perfect, but I wouldn't have chosen anyone else to grow up with. I love you both and am always here. To my sister Latrivia, thank you for encouraging me to take up this challenge.

To my family and friends, I love you all. This is only the beginning!!

PREFACE

Talk about what hurts you, what caused you to grow, what brings you joy, what brings you sorrow, what you hid, what you were told not to mention, how you feel, how you overcame, and how you stood. Don't allow anyone or anything to quiet your voice.

Talk About It

Talk about the things that make you cry,
The abuse that made you lie,
The betrayal that made you want to lay down
and die,
The lies that caused relationships to die,
The reasons behind the walls that you built, The
way that you learned to cope,
The things that have caused you to lose hope,
The death,
The bad choices,
The unspoken feelings,
The time that you were willing.
Talk about the joy,
Talk about the peace,
Talk about the love,
Talk about your dreams,
Talk about your fears,
Talk about your future,
Talk about today.
Talk about everything that you always wanted to
say.
TALK ABOUT IT
Because someone is listening,
Someone needs to hear it,
Someone knows how you feel,

Someone can help you,
Someone cares.

It's Dark in Here

It's dark in here, someone please turn on the
lights.
She's gone and it's all my fault, blaming myself
as if I have the power over life and death.
How do I live without her here? I'm hurting.
Who do I talk to? I'm so far away, I can't let
them see me cry.
What do I do?
It's dark in here, someone please turn on the
lights.
Someone touched me, ugh I know this isn't
right.
I don't like this feeling, but my body reacted.
I can't see!! **"open your eyes"**
You're hurting me!! **"open your eyes**."
Leave me alone!! **"open your eyes"**.
If you say something I will kill you,
No one will believe you!! **"open your eyes."**
It's dark in here, someone please turn on the
lights.
My body feels different, something isn't right.
I'm acting out,!! **" please turn on the lights."**
I hate my life!! **"Someone please turn on the
lights."**
 I don't have a future; this is the end of my life.

It's dark in here!! **"Someone please turn on the lights."**
Nothing excites me, my feelings are gone. The pain is overbearing, and they left me all alone. **Can someone please turn the lights on?**

Stuck

Don't stay stuck in a place that was not designed
for anyone to survive in.
Move forward even if you have to move blindly.
Hold your head up high and never look back.
Recognize the need to move and do so according
to what's best for you.
You can't survive if you can't breathe.
Stop for a moment and think about what it has
cost you to stay in this place.
Is it worth it?
Nothing is better than forward progress because
moving forward gets you close to your
destination.
It's so easy to become discouraged when you
have nothing motivating you or requiring you to
have courage.
Let you be enough, let life be enough, let being
tired be enough
The roller-coaster gets boring after you have
ridden it a few times!
You can sit back and pretend that you're fine but
the only one you are fooling is the one behind
your eyes. (YOU)
Sitting in the same place
Unmotivated to

Carry on
Knowing that you need to move.
It's time to Move.

The Single Mother

She gave birth to you, she raised you, she poured
into you, she did the best she could do
She feels like she failed, she's so overwhelmed,
she's stuck, she wants to give up
Her heart is broken, all the hateful words
unspoken
All she sees is what you could be
She blames herself every time you fail
"If I would have" is how her sentences begin
She didn't have instructions; she did the best she
could!!
She did what she thought was right, with no
signs of hope in sight
She was single, her help was limited
She wanted more but gave what she had
She stood beside you even when things looked
all bad
She was your voice until you formed your own
She cried for you, in her heart she died for you
She protected you the best way she could
She slowed down her dreams, changed her life
with only your life in sight
She made mistakes and caused some heartbreak
She lived life to give a life and did not think
twice

At times she felt alone but looking at you is
what made her strong
She found hope in your smile, she made a
promise to not let you down
It wasn't easy but she did it by herself
She's the strongest, the bravest, the most giving
In a world full of people who would have given
up she didn't
Cherish Her

I Just Don't Want To

I don't want to be who others expect me to be, I would rather be who I want to be. I would rather follow the beat that I hear in my head.
I don't want to use your lingo.
I don't want to wear your clothes.
I don't want to comb my hair in the styles that you approve of.
I don't need the car to validate my status. I don't want to hate them and love them.
I don't want to be the person you look up to for guidance.
I don't want to meet your expectations to be accepted.
I don't want to compromise ME to be part of WE.
I don't want to be part of the conversation.
I don't care about your in-crowd.
I laugh at your mean girl mentality or should I say, women. (We're grown)
I don't want to pretend.
I don't want to be one me when they're around and another when they're not.
I don't want to sit back and talk about those who don't have what I got.

I don't want to fake a smile pretending that I'm
ok when I'm not.
I don't want to color in the lines.
I don't want to make sure everyone else is ok all
while neglecting me.
I don't want to step outside of me just to be
accepted by you.
It's not that I can't, it's not that I'm afraid.
It's just that I DON'T WANT TO!!

Black People My People I Just Don't Get It

I don't get why our poor put themselves in debt
to look rich.
I don't get why our rich buy material things to
impress the poor.
I don't get why flashing your possessions is a
thing.
I don't get why those who struggle the most
spend the most.
I don't get why we continue to make the rich
man richer.
I don't get why we talk about the very thing we
dislike the most.
I don't get why we turn our people against each
other just for entertainment.
I don't get how you can say we matter and still
pull the trigger.
I don't get how we can scream free our family
then beg for the person who victimized our
family to be put in prison.
Where is their justice if your family member is
freed?
I don't get why we allow greed to take over us
and are willing to destroy anyone in our paths to
get what we want. (Even if it's us)

I don't get how we can be such an
embarrassment to our ancestors who fought so
hard to gain us a voice.
I don't get how we can live in a place that hates
us and still hate each other.
We expose our own all while covering up for
them, I don't get it.
I don't get how we can lead our youth astray all
while saying we are fighting for them.
I don't get how we stand stronger for others than
we do for ourselves.
We talk about justice but get a thrill out of street
fights, I don't get it.
We kill each other over blocks and
neighborhoods that we don't own, I don't get it.
We hate to see people in the same trade getting
along, I don't get it.
We build the beef and then judge the outcome; I
don't get it.
I wake up and I'm proud of being Black, I'm
proud of my big lips and nose, but when I look
at some of my people all I can say is, I DON'T
GET IT.
Can We Do Better??

Freedom

Freedom is a chain that I need to break Freedom
is a name that I can't forsake Freedom is the
vow that I refuse to break Freedom is doing it
for someone else's sake Freedom is the power
that you can't allow anyone else to take
Freedom is the mindset that we all must change
Freedom is a test that we must fail
Freedom is deeper than any cell
Freedom is the sound that we don't want to hear
Freedom is the pain that we all must bear
Freedom is the life that we must give
Freedom is the way that we must live Freedom
is the yes when we should say no Freedom is the
mountains that we must climb Freedom is not
leaving anyone behind Freedom is a word that
causes actions Freedom is walking away from
all our distractions
Freedom is the whisper that causes an uproar
Freedom is the slammed door
Freedom is not the answer, it's not the cause, it's
not the goal
Freedom only plays a small role
Freedom is not blaming it on FREEDOM

We See your Truth

Yeah, you're doing it, but you are only doing it
to be seen
You're putting in all this work, but your motives
aren't clean
You put the S on your chest but it's only for
show
You think you're winning but you're losing your
soul
You walk around with your crew so tight, but
couldn't even bust a grape in a fruit fight
You focused on the fame and everyone calling
your name, but you can't even stand on
everything you claim
Your heart is dark, you blend in with the night
but try to teach others how to be children of the
light.
Your mask is ripping we see your truth, don't try
to put it back on we know that's you
We hear your lies but see your truth The only
one you're fooling is you
Stop for a second think about what you're doing
No this doesn't mean your whole life is ruined
Change who you are, start working on you
because this behavior didn't just come up out of
the blue

We see you but do you see you? You know, the
real you
No more hiding, no more lying
Let's get better because your soul is dying, God
loves you
It's time for you to love you, You know, the real
you
We see your truth and now so do you
The change is coming it's time to work on you
The mask is gone, you're not alone
Let God in so he can save your soul

"I Still Have Work to Do"

I sit here in the midst of my hurt, confusion,
depression, fear, and hate.
I can't look left, I can't look right, I can't look
up, I can't look down.
Everything is dark. I can't breathe, **WHAT DO I
DO?**
I scream Lord Please, **I NEED YOU**
A still small voice says "**DAUGHTER**"
I felt chills. Everything stood still, my eyes
opened as tears started to fall.
God, I whispered **SILENCE**
God, I whispered **SILENCE**
GOD, I screamed
A still small voice says, "**Daughter STOP**".
GOD, I screamed as more tears fell.
All I hear is, "I will never leave you nor forsake
you. I'm always here to answer your call".
Daughter, "walk away your work is not done,
don't pull the trigger, put down that gun".
SILENCE
Peace fell over me and my hand dropped the
gun. At the edge of my defeat there He was
calling me his "daughter".
I want to live but my life is not worth living, I
want to live but not this life the world is giving,

I want to live **BUT I DON'T KNOW HOW.
WHAT NOW?**
I hate hurting, I hate being confused, I hate
being depressed, I hate being afraid, and I hate
feeling hateful.
But this is how I feel. What now?
"Seek Me", He says
As I sat weeping,
I felt hopeful, peace, joy, love, I felt wanted.
In that moment I knew that I still had work to
do.

Generational

Your mom did it, Her mom did it, Her mom did it, so now you have to do it
This is a lie!!
You don't have to follow in the footsteps of those who came before you
It's ok to create your own path and walk in it gracefully
What was for them was for them
Everybody talks about the generational curses and leave out the generational success
The good things the ones before you did, don't have to be your destiny either
We are breaking the curses and holding on to what we think is "worth it"
Those things have the potential to cause you to miss your true potential
We become so caught up in doing things the same way someone else did because we liked the results
What if God didn't intend on those being your results? What if he has something better for you?
Will you stay stuck in generational success and miss being blessed?
Explore the choices you have and create your own path

The Compromise

Compromise- a giving up to something that is wrong or degrading
We compromise to fit in; I know what I'm doing is wrong, but everyone around me is doing it
We compromise to be accepted; I know they wouldn't like who I really am so I put on a mask to look like something they would like
We compromise to be loved; I accept things I don't like just so they won't walk out of my life
We compromise to live; I can't find a job so I can just do this to get a quick buck.
We compromise because we're hurt; Because they did this to me, I'm going to do this to hurt them (you're hurting you)
We compromise to fill a void; Maybe if I do this I will fill better
It's so easy to compromise because compromising doesn't cause us to self-reflect instead, we self-neglect. We neglect the small voice that says, STOP, WALK AWAY, THEY DON'T LOVE YOU, YOU'RE HURTING, DON'T DO THAT, and HEAL. Because we are afraid to face our own insecurities, we live according to the false securities of our delusions.

It's time to turn Compromise into Promise.
Promise- a cause or ground for hope
We have to promise to be good to ourselves;
Yes, they hurt me but I'm not going to allow the
things that hurt me to control my life
We have to promise to be aware; I know this
isn't right so let me walk away or not engage for
my safety.
We have to promise ourselves to heal; After all
that I have been through God, please deliver me.
We have to promise to allow God to come in and
heal, set free, and deliver us
The key to reaching the promise (finding hope)
is in God, nothing or no one else

Truth

The truth is you're not ok you just pretend to be that way; you hid between the lies of the things you've sacrificed
The truth is you haven't healed; you cry at night when you think no one is listening
The truth is you're lost; you pretend that you have it all together, but you really don't know where you are going
The truth is you want to die; but you live because you believe you have people counting on you
The Truth is you haven't been introduced to the real truth
The truth is you are ok because Jesus paid the ultimate sacrifice so no matter what you have done God will forgive you.
The truth is your healing is in God, seek His face, get in His word, and allow Him to heal your soul.
The truth is the word of God is your road map; open it to find directions.
The truth is you want to live but you just don't know how. Be born again so that you can live again.

The truth is in God and His word is the key to
life
Unlock the truth

Invisible

Can you look at me? Will you look at me? Can
you see me? Hello!
In a room full of people and no one sees me. Am
I here? HELLO!
You can't see me hurting
You don't see my swollen eyes from the nightly
cries
You don't see the cuts on my wrist from the
suicide attempts
HELLO! Are you there?
Can you hear me scream as I sit next to you
quietly?
Can you smell the blood from my bleeding
heart?
In a room full of people and no one sees me
HELLO!
You can't tell that I haven't left the house in
three days
You didn't notice how my hair has looked for
the last three weeks
You don't see the blisters on my feet from
walking all night barefoot on the concrete hello!
Now that I'm gone everyone sees me, they cry at
night because I took my life.

They share memories that we shared. During
those times I felt as if no one cared. I felt alone,
scared, sad, mad, wishing someone would ask
ARE YOU OK!
I sat around in those big crowds alone, but now
that I'm going everyone is telling them to be
strong. Providing the comfort that I missed. I felt
invisible. I didn't think they saw me.
Did they see me? Was I there?
Did they really care?
They talk "to me" and "reference me" now more
than they did when I was there with them. What
is this? What has gotten into them?
They say I should have told them that I wasn't
ok, but my pain didn't work that way.
They could have asked instead every time I
acted out, they said "just relax."
They ignored my silent cries and now they say
how hard my death has impacted their lives.
One, "I see you" would have saved me!!!
Instead, I was Invisible. BUT my death made me
visible!!
(Pay attention to the nonverbal signs)

More than

She is more than what you thought she would be
More than what your shallow eyes could see
She's more than the lies
More than the failed tries
More than you wishing she would die More than
the pain
More than the weight gain
She's more than what you speak, she already
surpassed what you think
She's more than the lust
More than the heartbreak and distrust
She's more than the times you would watch her
lay down and sob
More than the job
More than the funny pics and the bad butt job
She's more than the fame
More than the popular name She's more than a
wife
She's far more than what you can define her as
in this life
More than the title
More than the one that some idol
She became more than what you know once God
got a hold of her and saved her soul

So, cherish her, love her, esteem her, and
remember God allowed you to have her and to
Him, she is more than what you could ever
think!!

Just a Thought

Following the instructions, believing in my heart
that I can trust him.
WAITING AND ANTICIPATING,
ANXIOUS!!
Standing tall knowing that he will get me
through it all.
Even if I have a major fall, he will pick me up.
My winning isn't luck, and my failing doesn't
mean I wasn't able.
It's all in his timing so if I win or if I lose it's all
working for my good.
I DON'T CARE ABOUT THE OPINIONS OF
OTHERS!!
Walking around defeated isn't the purpose
because the things that God does go beneath the
surface.
His plan for me is what's best for me, he is the
one who created me.
I might not like what I see but the seen is not my
focus.
My eyes are blurred because the lines are
blurred.
He goes outside of the lines beyond the eyes.
Working for my good, so that He can get the
glory.

It might not make sense, it might not seem possible, but stand on His word and believe it in your soul.

HE IS MOVING!

Being sidetracked can get you off track but allow God to bring you right back.

Life isn't life unless you're living it with him. The failure, the success, the sadness, the joy, the reaping and sowing it all works out for his glory. You can live the "good" life where you go home and weep every night

OR

You can live the Godly life where the JOY in your spirit refreshes your soul and even the bad days turn into joy.

You can only fake for so long. Eventually, the hurt in your heart will bleed through your clothes.

In Him, you find true peace, joy, comfort, and answers.

Let's live for God and dismiss those worldly masters.

Don't mind me, this was just a thought!!

I'm Different

I'm Different, I walk in it, I talk in it
I don't look like your average woman, and I
don't plan to
I don't want to fall into the expectations of this
world
I don't have to agree with the boy on boy or girl
on girl
I don't have to be excited to see you every time I
see you, I love you but that's just not me
I don't have to sound or look like them, I'm
happy with who I am
And trust me I know whose I am
I'm not living up to the standards of this world
because the bible tells me I'm in the world but
not of it
I can wear my natural hair, no make-up and still
be beautiful
I don't have to get made up when I wake up I'm
different because I choose to be
I don't have to impress anyone but the one who
created me (GOD)
If you can't accept my difference, then step
away because it won't make a difference

I don't know when I'm going to die but I don't
want to leave here stuck because I lived a lie;
I'm Different

Come Back

Just because you walked away doesn't mean you
can't come back
Kill your pride your life is on the line Ok, they
hurt you
Yes, they lied
But Did God?
You walked away from the only person that
could get you through everything you are facing,
just to hurt
In your face all you see is hurt, pain, resentment,
and hate
Let Go
Free yourself so you can be yourself
You know Him!!
He's calling you back
There is nothing that he did to make you turn
your back
He saved you, He protected you, He comforted
you, and even provided for you
Find your way back to Him, don't let your life
be hard because of the likes of them
You feel different, you live different, you even
hate different
Listen to his voice, I WILL NEVER LEAVE
YOU NOR FORSAKE YOU!!

Has he forsaken you?
No, but they did
How long does God have to pay for the choices
that man has made?
Turn Back, Come Back, Get your life BACK
It's ok to not be ok, He knew that you would feel
this way
How can he heal you if he's not who you go to?
Call on Him, Come Back to Him, You need Him
Your life isn't over, He's still there to give you
His shoulder!
Cry Out instead of trying to hide out
SO WHAT, He forgives you for that too
Come Back

See Color

See color because we are all different
See color because we all have different shades
See color because the colors highlight beauty
See color because color makes us who we are
See color because mines might be unique
See color, but don't label me as a freak
See color but don't treat me different based on it
See color but don't allow it to change your
perception of me
See color but don't separate me because mines
are different
See color because when we look in the mirror
that's one thing we see
See color because my color is part of me
See color because it's and inheritance
See color but don't try to change it
See color but don't make it all you see
See color because it exists

Walk

The hardest thing you will ever have to do is
walk away from you
Walk away from your excuses
Walk out of your comfort zone
Walk away from your feelings
Walk away from your opinions
Walk away from what you thought you knew
Walk away from your false truth
Walk away from your "friends"
Walk away from your attitude
Walk away from the walls you build
Walk away from the reality you made
Walk away from the time you waste
Walk away from the beliefs you hold
Walk away from the tied souls
But the best thing you could do is walk away
from you
And walk into the will of God
Walk into His comfort
Walk into His thoughts and opinions
Walk into Biblical truths
Walk into the relationship with Him
Walk into His reality
Walk into the gifts He holds
Walk into a brand-new soul

Walk into the freedom from you and the Life
with Him
And while you're walking bring a friend or two

I Woke Up

I woke up to a feeling that my fourteen-year-old
body never felt.
I woke up being told to shut up, nobody will
believe you.
I woke up crying because internally I was dying.
I woke up scared alone, afraid, and intimidated.
I woke up sad, mad, and angry.
I woke up LOST.
I woke up drowning.
I woke up in disbelief.
I woke up full of grief.
I woke up hoping and praying that I wouldn't.
Every time I woke up, I could smell the scent,
feel the feeling, hear the words.
Every time I felt the pain.
I woke up trying to self-destruct.
I woke up trying to die.
I woke up numb.
I woke up
I WOKE UP
Thirteen Years later
I woke up to joy, peace, and love.
I woke up filled with God's love.
I woke up wanting to live.
I woke up wanting to love.

I woke up forgiving.
I woke up repenting.
I woke FREE.
I woke up ME.
I WOKE UP

How Are You Living??

It is very important that we: young, old, black, white, etc. live our lives to our fullest potential. It is so easy to get caught up in the fear of failing.
Failing is part of the experience, so take the risk. If we trust God in the process, risks turn into faith. I can't see it, but I know through Christ I can do it. Reaching milestones and continuing is the best way to experience life. Some say we only live once but if you live in God, you never die. So, life continues after life. After you have rested, you will be revived. But, how can you know if you never pick up and go? Spread God's word, save some souls, plant some seeds, and watch them grow. Your life produces what you water. If you water fear, you will live a fearful life. It also depends on the type of water you're using, are you using living water or still water? The still water keeps you still doing the very things that you have been doing for years. The living water gives your life and life produces life.

Who are you to say who's wrong and who's right if your right isn't predicated on God's sight? I can live in my wrongs and never move forward, or I can bask in what's right and live a fruitful life. Sometimes we get so caught up in others that we forget to live for ourselves. Think about it, are their opinions more important than you living? Because I'm not grammatically correct will your day be ruined? So, you can correct my grammar but ignore my cry for help. Will gossiping about me benefit you? So, you see where I fall short and instead of helping you kick me while I'm down? Am I all over the place or are you just not in the right headspace?

How can you live your life to its fullest potential if you don't even know you have potential? You don't know the word of God, you have never read scripture, you never heard His voice, and no one around you has spoken life into you. What do you do? You stand up and search for the truth. The truth is in God. It's not something you run to, so you look ok. It's something you run to, to be ok. Will you live for today because you can't see tomorrow? Or will you live chasing every tomorrow? Having the same blurred lines making plans for days that you don't even own. Or will you wake up in the morning and sing a new song? Live right today because you might not have a tomorrow.